GW00359418

The publishers would like to express their gratitude to Roadstone Dublin Ltd, Kingscourt Brick, Waterford Stanley and the Heritage Council whose generosity made this publication possible.

Near Edenderry, Co. Offaly, this cosy house is tucked out of the way. Although the house is at least 150 years old, the people in the locality were able to point out the hole from which the clay was taken.

Ireland's Earthen Houses

Frank McDonald and Peigín Doyle
Photographs by Hugh MacConville

Published by A. & A. Farmar

Published by
A. & A. Farmar
Beech House
78 Ranelagh Village
Dublin 6
Ireland

Acknowledgements
Many people and organisations contributed to the publication of this work. We would particularly like to thank Kingscourt Brick, Roadstone Dublin, Waterford Stanley and the Heritage Council; the owners of the houses featured in this book for their hospitality and patience when their homes were being photographed; the Garda Síochána in Monasterevin; Dominic Berridge, Co. Wexford; John Munn, Stella Maris Centre, Kilmore Quay; Bairbre Ní Fhloinn, Department of Irish Folklore, University College Dublin; David Griffin and the staff of the Irish Architectural Archive; Michael Higginbotham, Office of Public Works; Dick Oram, Department of the Environment, Northern Ireland; Jane Richard, School of Architecture, Plymouth; Ned Culleton, Des MacConville, Una MacConville and Cormac MacConville; Leo Casey, Mayglass, Co. Wexford.

Contents

In the rich market garden country of Rush, north Co. Dublin, this house seems to rise out of the soil around it. Now nearly surrounded by modern housing, it shows how at peace with its surroundings it is compared to many newer buildings in the area.

Preface by Hugh MacConville

I first heard of the great Irish tradition of mud-built houses when some people I knew wanted to build a house on a site a relation had given them in north Co. Dublin. It was in the early 1970s, around the time of the first oil crisis. With the need to save energy in mind, the young couple and their architect set out to build the most energy-efficient house possible. They found that mud or marly clay, a traditional building material in the area, was the most energy-efficient material for building. It was freely available and houses built with it were warm in winter and cool in summer. So the project became exciting, not only from an energy conservation point of view but also because it had an added dimension of historical continuity.

When the relation was given the great news that the house was to be made from

Near Monasterevin, Co. Kildare, this building in the local style has a warmth and pride about it. Clay houses don't always have hipped roofs but this style is very common in Co. Kildare.

mud, he reacted very badly. He told the young people that it had taken his family long enough to get out of a mud cabin and he was not going to see the next generation going back into one, not on his land anyway!

A lot has changed since then. Nearly all the people I met in the last two years, while travelling around the country taking photographs of their houses for this book, are extremely proud of their homes and delighted to share one of Ireland's best-kept architectural secrets.

Each area seems to have its own style, just as there are different styles of fiddle-playing in different areas. It would have been a tragedy if traditional music had never been collected and was lost to us: we will be much the poorer if we fail to cherish our clay buildings with all their vitality and diversity, and the insight they give us into the lives of those who lived in them.

The Building Blocks of Ireland

For our ancestors, the transport of heavy building materials from a distance was generally quite impractical for all but the wealthiest, so they were constrained to use local materials. These were—stone, clay, sods, grass, straw and timber. The type and quality of these simple building materials varied widely; in some places they were plentiful and easy to handle, in others a great deal of work was required for the simplest building.

The least expensive, and by far the most common form of construction, was the sod-wall cabin. This consisted simply of large grassy lumps cut from the earth. A foundation of loose stones was laid, and the trimmed sods, usually about 2 feet by 3 feet in size, were piled up to form the wall. The resultant walls were weak and very apt to subside, even when supported by timber uprights. Where suitable timber was available, pegs or twigs might be used to peg one course to another; sometimes the sods were mortared together with clay. Window and door openings were created simply by hacking out a suitable space with a hay-knife once the building was

---

Vernacular building materials

Sods	the cheapest and most common building material—now obsolete
Drystone	used in parts of the West, nowadays only for walling
Mud	the second most common material to be seen today
Mortared stone	the most common material
Timber	hardly used since the sixteenth century
Brick	used in towns but rarely in the country

---

complete. The roof was typically supported by corner posts. A sod-wall house could be erected in a day.

The next most common material was mud or clay, the subject of this book. Its use in Ireland can be traced back to Anglo-Norman times, and even earlier to the wattle and daub houses of Viking Ireland. Clay buildings survive best in warm, dry areas and remains can be found nearly everywhere in Ireland apart from the wet and windy western coasts of most of Donegal, Mayo, Galway and south-west Cork and Kerry, the classic drystone areas.

Drystone construction can be seen at its best in the Dingle peninsula, where the Gallarus oratory remains watertight 1,000 year after its erection. Less skilled builders elsewhere generally used turf to fill the gaps between the stones.

At the time the clay houses were originally erected, mud—being durable, affordable, warm in winter and cool in summer—was the chosen material for a strong farmer's house. Arthur Young declared in *A Tour in Ireland 1776-9* that such buildings were 'far warmer than the thin clay walls in England . . . their inhabitants [are] as well off as most English cottagers.' However, just as neglect and poverty turned the fine Georgian town houses of Mountjoy Square and Gardiner Street into slums so, too, clay houses fell into disrepute. The material was tainted by the fate of the people living in the houses.

A recently renovated clay house in Drumcree, Co. Westmeath

Comparative costs of a cabin made of sods, mud and stone in the 18th century—from Arthur Young's Tour in Ireland 1776–9

Cost of a sod cabin in Fermanagh	£2
Cost of a mud cabin in Roscommon	£5 5s
Cost of a stone and slate cabin in Roscommon	£15

This Co. Wexford farmhouse, which is substantial even by today's standards, must have been very important in the locality 250 years ago. The building is a mixture of clay and stone.

Earthen Houses by Frank McDonald

For centuries, most people in rural Ireland housed themselves in small cabins, made from whatever materials were most plentifully available in the locality. In the West, for obvious reasons, these houses were made from stone but in the Midlands and along the east coast, where stone was not so readily available, clay was the favoured material, even for quite large houses. The 1841 Census showed that nearly half of rural Ireland's population was living in this type of house which it divided into four classes— first the 'gentleman's residence', second, the larger farmhouses, third the smaller farmhouses and lastly, 'houses built of mud or other perishable material having only one room and window'.

The latter category would have included the poorest and most common type of dwelling, the sod-built house. Clay

Near Duleek, Co. Meath

houses were a step up from these, and required considerable labour to erect. Before building work started the site would be marked out by placing flat stones at the corners, each with a smaller stone on top, to be left there overnight. If the stones were still in place on the following day, construction could begin with some confidence. This unusual tradition had its roots in fairy folklore. Essentially, every housebuilder had to make sure that he was not about to erect his dwelling across a path used by the 'good people', or *slua sí* of Irish mythology. In effect, by placing their stones in position, they were applying to the fairies for planning permission. (Farmers also took care not to damage clumps of trees in the middle of a field, as well as ringforts and other prehistoric remains, for the same reason; it was only after the advent of intensive agriculture, following Ireland's entry into the European Community in 1973, that some of them began to show a reckless disregard for inconveniently-located archaeological sites.)

Making a clay house began by mixing the marly sub-soil excavated for its foundations. Chopped straw was added to the mix as it was turned over and sprinkled with water, then it was left to 'sour' for a few days to absorb the moisture. The labour required to knead the thick, sticky clay was very great—'it would pull the ribs out of a man' the folklorist Caomhín Ó Danachair was told by one of his inform-ants. More water was sprinkled on the mix and it was again left to sour for a few more days until it was sufficiently firm to use as a building material; the test was whether it could stand 18 inches wide and a foot deep without bulging. By then the stone foundations, usually nine inches deep and rising another nine inches above ground level, would have been laid, unevenly at the top to provide a 'key' for the clay.

The mud walls were raised using a graip or sprong—a long-handled implement with three or four long, flat metal prongs at the end. This was used to manipulate the clay, patting it down to improve its adhesive properties and subse-

Three stages of neglect

This building, located on the Dublin/Meath border at Clonee, will soon be engulfed by the suburbs of west Dublin. The owners of many pubs and shopping centres in the suburbs and satellite towns around Dublin are trying to invent a past for themselves with clock-towers and mock Victoriana. It would be lovely to see a building like this playing a role in any new development in the area.

Standing beside the main Dublin/Belfast road, this derelict house is an example of what remains of the country's stock of clay houses. The owner said that Fingal County Council were encouraging him to knock the building down. Enlightened man that he is, he refused.

Travellers on the road to the West will be familiar with this building near Enfield, Co. Meath. It was once a house, then a cow house, and now it is returning to the earth. It is sad to see it go but it is a fine example of a recyclable building (apart from the galvinised sheeting).

quently in 'paring', or shaving, the wall. Parings were not wasted, however; they were thrown back into the heap of soured mud and mixed in with it. The walls were built up in layers—sometimes using boards or shutters—until they reached a height of six-and-a-half feet. Windows and door openings were created either by inserting wooden frames in the wall and building up on each side and over the top—often without any strengthening such as a lintel would provide—or by filling the intended opes with turf sods which could be knocked out easily when the building was finished.

Chimneys were constructed on the mud cross wall which divided smaller houses into two rooms. In the better houses, these were raised in stone. But many builders relied on using strong pieces of rough timber through which holes were bored five or six inches apart and filled with standard rods of willow or hazel. Then the whole frame was interlaced with wicker-work and plastered over with a mixture of daub and cow manure to form a 'good chimney', perhaps four feet wide

Bremore Cottage, just north of Balbriggan, Co. Dublin. Reckoned to be one of the largest thatched houses in Ireland, it was maliciously set on fire some years ago.

and three feet deep at the lower end tapering to a foot-square opening, plastered and whitewashed, on the ridge line of the cabin. Often, clay was combined with wattle or straw rope to make hearth canopies. Rough, rather than sawn timber was used to form the roof, which was usually hipped or half-hipped, and thatched with straw or reeds or, in the case of poorer dwellings, rushes or heather.

Though built of clay, this type of house in the baronies of Forth and Bargy in Co. Wexford was described by the *Irish Farmers' Journal* in 1814 as 'neat, cleanly and commodious; stone is not to be had here without great expense, but the surprising expertness with which this substitute is handled, and moulded into habitable form, makes a quarry altogether unnecessary. With a compost of moistened clay and straw, without plumb, square or level, but merely with an instrument they call a

Kilmore Quay in Co. Wexford has a fine collection of thatched houses. The community is promoting this as one of the village's attractions.

sprong . . . every man is capable of erecting a house for himself, compact and perpendicular'. Only the scale varied with the circumstances of the proprietor, whether affluent or poor.

More thatched mud houses have survived in Co. Wexford than almost anywhere else. One of them is in the townland of Pollwitch, near Mayglass and not far from Johnstown Castle, which is dealt with in detail by Peigín Doyle in the last chapter of this book. A feature in the *Wexford People* a few years ago noted that a team of University College Dublin academics 'spent a day drooling over the place' and returned to Dublin 'having photographed every nook and cranny' of the two-storey house, which dates from the early 18th century. The fireplace alone was 'a monument to a way of life which has been all but erased', its mud brick chimney radiating a form of central heating throughout the house.

In 1942, during the Emergency, Frank Gibney—father of Arthur, the gold medal award-winning architect—made a modest proposal to the Industrial Research Council, suggesting that people should be encouraged to build in clay because of its widespread availability. He also argued that clay-built houses, in terms of their design, construction and insulation properties, were 'superior to many of our modern, standardised thin-walled cottages'. The only impediment to reviving the ancient art that he could see was a 'psychological one, for public opinion may appear hesitant in considering an idea associated with "mud cabins", peasantry and poverty'.

Gibney sent the Industrial Research Council a hand-made block of marl clay 'taken from a depth of 18 inches below top-soil level in my own garden at Sutton, Co. Dublin'. He proposed that a few experimental houses could be erected in

On the Wexford/Gorey road, this building of clay and stone is in the Wexford style of two-storey, high-roofed houses.

the Lusk area where numerous clay-built houses still existed at that time. 'Granted attainment of hygienic standards, the thick and white-walled clay-built cottage, long and low, hugging the soil from whence it sprang and capped with its rolling roof of thatch, could remain a characteristic feature of the Irish landscape', he wrote. However, the prejudice against this most vernacular building type was so entrenched that his plea fell on deaf ears.

It would be impossible to exaggerate the pervasive nature of this prejudice; it is part of our cultural baggage. As long ago as 1878, an article in *The Irish Builder* entitled 'The Mud Cabin in History and Architecture', perfectly encapsulates the received wisdom about the housing conditions in rural Ireland during the 19th century. 'Though still not half so plentiful as in our younger days, the mud cabins in several counties in Ireland are still, alas!, too plentiful', it said, adding that it seemed as if these 'barbarous relics of the past' would continue to exist 'until the landed proprietors of the country are forced through very shame to replace them, or stand self-convicted as enemies of national morality and public health'.

So imbued was *The Irish Builder* by the culture of Victorian improvement that it sought to have these 'miserable constructions' swept away, to be

Wexford farmhouses are famous for their neatness. This beautifully maintained house in Wexford is a perfect example of how clay walls can be shaped.

replaced by 'a better class of human dwellings in stone, brick and concrete materials'. The highly-respected journal recognised, however, that this was unlikely to happen immediately, so it also put forward a number of ideas about how the construction of mud or clay cabins could be improved, to alleviate dampness and structural instability, while still making use of traditional materials.

Yet, even today, it has been estimated that earth structures embrace some 30 per cent of the world's population, housing no fewer than 1.7 billion people. Sixty per cent of houses in Peru are made from moulded bricks or rammed earth, as well as more than 70 per cent of India's housing stock and 38 per cent of the houses in Kigali, the capital of Rwanda. According to Hugo Houben, a French architect based in Grenoble, up to 90 per cent of the houses in some villages in the Dauphine region are earth dwellings, while there were 200,000 adobe (sun-dried earth brick) houses in California in 1980 and the use of this material was growing at the rate of 30 per cent a year.

'From the very humblest shelters to the multi-form granaries of Africa, from the palaces of the Hausa emirs of Nigeria to the ksours and kasbahs of Morocco, from the mosques of Mali to the tightly-packed neighbourhoods of Isfahan in Iran, from the fortified dwellings of the Najran area of Saudi Arabia to the 10-storey or more earth blocks of Shibam, in Yemen, from the moulded brick farms of Acquitaine to the baroque and neo-classical castles of the Saone valley, from the pueblos of the New Mexico Indians to the houses in concentric rings of the Hakkas of the province of Fujian, in China, the whole world bears the indelible stamp of earthen architecture'.

Though the use of mud had regressed over the past 50 years in more industrialised countries, Houben told the 1995 'Out of Earth' conference in Plymouth that it had continued unabated elsewhere, especially in the developing world. 'Burdened by debt and confronted by an urgent need to build on a scale unprecedented in history, building with earth emerges as one of the efficient, short-term means of production of housing and public facilities

Solar heating may be a relatively new term but the builder of this house 200 years ago created the ultimate solar house. Facing south/south-east, the clay walls collect the heat of the sun during the day and, like a storage heater, release it at night.

On the Dublin/Meath border this house, renovated in the 1950s, and possibly 150 years old, is still a successful building.

(schools, for example)'. The material is widely available locally, it is economical to use and has the additional advantage of being both culturally and climatically suitable—in other words, it represents the essence of 'sustainable development'.

Enumerating its environmental advantages, Houben pointed out that unbaked earth does not contribute to the deforestation which follows the use of timber for firing bricks; it does not consume any non-renewable energy, such as oil or gas, in the production of materials; it does not require transportation, being available locally; it does not contribute to a degradation of the landscape, as the earth excavated for roads can be recycled as a building material; it does not contribute to diminishing resources, such as sand and gravel; it uses very little water, so precious to people's lives, especially in Africa, and it produces no industrial or chemical waste.

In Britain, the realisation in the past decade that earthen buildings form an important part of the national heritage, led to the implementation of a research programme at the University of Plymouth by the Centre for Earthen Architecture, headed by Rex Harries. The programme aims to develop a set of 'best practice' techniques for building in earth and to develop guidelines for an inventory of earth buildings. An area within a 10-kilometre radius of Crediton, in mid-Devon, was selected for a pilot of its villages, hamlets and farms, and uses a variety of soil types reflecting the area's geology.

Britain has tens of thousands of mud-walled, or cob, buildings—mostly in the southwest of England. 'After cob was dismissed earlier this century in favour of mass-produced bricks and concrete, this most green of building methods is coming back into favour', reported the London *Times* in July, 1995. The revivalist movement has been spearheaded by the Devon Earth Building Society, which is trying to get across the message that mud houses are far from squalid and substandard. 'The result is a building that breathes, has no condensation problem and has good insulation, making it cool in summer and cosy in winter', wrote Jenny McClean.

The article featured an attractive four-bedroom clay house built by Kevin McCabe near Coylton, in east Devon. 'The materials he used could not be more indigenous: 70 tons of soil from his back garden, mixed with 30 tons of locally quarried silt and stones to reduce shrinkage, and 120 bales of straw from nearby farms. The roof is thatch, but this material is less important than a good overhang, he says. "With a roof over the cob walls, the house will last for 1,000 years . . . The lovely thing about cob is that it looks organic; and it looks like it has been here forever".' And because of its good insulation properties, the McCabe family's fuel bill for the previous winter was just £200.

Larry Keefe, a retired conservation officer with Teignbridge District Council in Devon and secretary of the Earth Building Society, has produced a guide to the repair and maintenance of clay buildings for Devon Historical Buildings Trust. He also sees them as organic, using natural materials derived directly from the surrounding landscape. 'Like any organism, they must—in order to remain healthy—

be able to breathe' and to respond readily to variations in temperature and humidity. In seeking to bring cob buildings up to modern standards by "improvement" or alteration, the greatest care must be taken to avoid works which might upset this balance with the environment'.

In the Czech Republic, Slovakia and Hungary, there is also a growing interest in earthen architecture. Despite the collectivisation of agriculture during the Communist period, a large number of houses made of unbaked earth still exist in rural areas, notably in Moravia and southern Slovakia, and many of these are listed for preservation because of their intrinsic value as vernacular buildings. They are also very well-documented, having been the subject of numerous academic studies from the late-19th century onwards; ethnographers searching for an authentic 'national style' of architecture were particularly interested in this form of construction.

At the Technical University of Brno, capital of Moravia, architecture and engineering students have collaborated to produce designs for new earthen buildings, as a way of solving ecological problems. The desire to preserve and record this part of the province's heritage, led to the establishment of an open-air museum at Straznice, in southern Moravia. 'Most of the structures built in this museum are copies; the originals still exist and are protected by law *in situ*', Zuzana and Jiri Syrova told the Plymouth conference in 1995. They also noted that raw earth continued to be used as a building material until the 1950s, after experiencing a revival in the wake of World War II.

The Hungarian Open Air Museum at Szentendre also features earthen buildings 'transplanted' from all parts of the country, like the Ulster Folk and Transport Museum in Cultra, Co. Down. But unlike Bunratty Folk Park in Co. Clare, where tourism rules the roost, Hungary's open air museum has become a centre for scientific research into the country's rich tradition of vernacular architecture, still very strong today. It contains the largest archives of folk architecture in Hungary, including thousands of survey reports, photographs, videotapes and more than 100,000 pages of verbal information or observations put on record, according to its director, Dr Miklos Cseri.

In Ireland, however, we place little or no value on our own vernacular architecture, still less on thatched mud or clay houses. We have been turning our backs on them for so long that they have become almost invisible. State aid for the relatively few that survive is minimal and confined to small grants towards re-thatching; the intrinsic value of the house itself is largely unrecognised, and unlike Devon, there is no effective lobby for their preservation and relatively little academic or technical research which might provide practical assistance to their owners on how to maintain this valuable, and irreplaceable, link with out past.

As we get on with building modern bungalows in the countryside, with PVC porticos and landscaped gardens borrowed from suburbia, is it not too much to hope that we might save what is left of where we came from?

The Fine Detail of Doors and Windows

Kilmore Quay

The Mayglass Farmstead, Pollwitch—a 250 Year-old Survivor
by Peigín Doyle

Although a little rundown now, the Mayglass farmstead exudes an ancient sense of snug comfort and ease. The house stands with its back to the sea winds, as it has for 250 years—at a comfortable height for human perspective, neither too squat nor dwarfing the viewer. Its walls are overhung with oaten thatch, its rounded outline shows the pleasing imperfection of something that is hand-built rather than factory-made.

This is an earthen house. Houses very like it were plentiful once, but the one in Mayglass is special because its interior has scarcely been changed for at least a hundred years, and because of the insight it provides into the people who built such houses and the manner in which they lived.

The house was built, according to local memory, in either 1703 or 1723. It was a family home through 1798, the Great Famine and all the social and political upheavals since. Many features of the house mark it out as the home of people who had taste, skills, a reasonable income and who lived far enough above subsistence to have had the time to embellish their home. The very fact that it survived so long shows it was a home to value and take care of.

Its last owner, Seamus Kirwan, then in his eighties, died only recently. His family came to the house in 1913, having bought it from the previous owners, the Blakes. It still retains many features which would have been common a hundred and more years ago.

You enter this now uninhabited house through a porch door into a small hallway facing a blank wall. There is a half-door with curved top, so the main door could be left open and the half-door closed, depending on the weather. The blank facing wall is one side of an enormous fireplace which stretches nearly the width of the kitchen, the main room. (This so-called 'jamb-wall' protecting the central fireplace from the winds coming through the front door is characteristic of many such houses.) To the left is a steep staircase, leading to two upper bedrooms behind the chimney breast.

The kitchen itself is one and a half storeys high, reaching to the bare thatch of the roof. The roof rests on the mud and stone walls which are about 10 feet high and 18 feet at the gable. The thatched roof is supported by rafters (couples) of stripped tree trunks to which it is joined

The fireplace and its chimney dominate the house in Mayglass. The clay bricks retain heat, and distribute it around the whole building.

by twisted straw ropes, some of which must date from the 18th century. Dangling by twine from the thatch are little paper packets, containing quantities of leftover seeds. It is a high ceilinged, spacious room, dominated by an enormous fireplace, and lit by two windows, in the front and back walls.

The fireplace is the main feature of the room and is built of unfired clay bricks in such a way that the clay retains the heat and distributes it around the house. The chimney is the width of the fireplace and narrows slightly as it rises to the roof. Peer up and you see the sky and the chimney wall.

The front chimney breast is supported by a beam about a foot thick and six foot wide, stretching across the width of the chimney. It curves downward slightly on one side, like the prow of a boat. It is reputed to be a ship's timber, possibly salvaged from the coast a few miles away and brought here when the house was being built. It was common for people in this area to go to Tacumshin Lake to salvage timber. Each person would have

The old Mayglass farmstead as it is today

their own pile of wood on the shore, which would be respected by his neighbours. The chimney breast itself is a triangular wall of clay bricks which tapers inwards and stretches upwards to join the thatch-ceiling.

Set snugly within the fireplace on either side are two wooden benches, where the family could sit cosy and secure from draughts. Not that there were many, for the whole house is dry and warm, even without a fire. An oven has been built into the wall and over the fireplace is a crane, from which an old black iron kettle is suspended.

Against the back wall of the kitchen is a wooden 'fiddle-front' dresser, so called because of the shape of the wooden partitions between the two press doors. The dresser is set on a plinth made of clay, the same material as the floor, and the bottom presses are separated by a clay partition built out from the wall. On its upper shelves is an array of jugs, mugs, bowls and dishes, many with flower and leaf designs that are generations old. There are oil lamps and candle sticks. Hanging

The warm, dark interiors of the old house glow with a secret life.

on the gable wall is a wooden kneading tray and wire mesh food cover. Beside the dresser is a small table, also holding crockery. A neighbour recalls that, as a child, he was sent by his mother to buy milk, eggs and butter from the family and the ha'pennies, pennies and threepenny bits for the transactions would be held in two pottery bowls on this dresser.

A small sash window in the back wall is covered by a lace curtain and an inside shutter of light wood. On the floor beneath the window is the wheel of a bellows which until recently fanned the fire. These are common enough, but beside the wheel is a rare feature– a wooden damper set into the floor. If the damper is lifted, a draught of air from outside the house blows in, again to ventilate the fire. There are four altogether in the room, at different angles to the fireplace, so there is ventilation no matter what direction the wind is blowing. The floor is hardened clay, which was dug out and replaced from time to time.

To the right of the front door, behind the massive fireplace, is a middling sized parlour, with its own fireplace, wooden floor and panelled doors and shutters. The fireplace is dark stained wood. Set into the angle of the wall is a full length cupboard, called a Cupid's Bow cupboard, because of the shape of the front of the shelves. An aperture in the clay wall on the other side of the fireplace forms another small cupboard, about a foot square, with its own wooden door. In the parlour, as in all the rooms, are a number of holy pictures, but over the mantelpiece are also a large framed tinted photograph of a lady in nineteenth-century dress, the mother of the last resident, and a framed coloured print of Charles Stewart Parnell. A table and some turned wood chairs complete the furnishings.

There's a woman's touch to be seen here. Two embroidered pictures, in cross-stitch, of a crucifix and religious motto and a religious scene, adorn the walls. The ceilings here and in the two rooms beyond the parlour are plastered.

Two doors lead from the parlour, one to a small bedroom at the gable end opposite the kitchen. It has wooden flooring over a clay base, an iron bedstead, and small wash table and mirror. Lace curtains and panelled shutters frame the sash window. Over the washstand is another cupboard excavated out of the clay wall.

The second door leads to a small, narrow room, like a pantry. This was the dairy. Lit by a small sash window, with clay floor, it is cool and well ventilated. There are bowls and buckets on the floor and shelves, a dash churn, narrow table, and two large, wide-lipped pottery bowls, possibly used for holding milk and cream.

Steep kitchen stairs lead to the upstairs bedrooms. There is a small landing at the top of the stairs where the low thatch forces one to bend before entering the bedroom.

The first bedroom is behind the chimney wall, with wooden floors and partition, open thatch ceiling and a sash window at floor level. The bed is iron framed, a lilac-coloured patchwork quilt is draped on the bedstead, and there is a small chest of drawers. The room is spacious, stretching the width of the house, but the roof which joins the walls at floor level is A-shaped, forcing one to

bend to look out the window. Apart from the chest of drawers, everything is stored in wooden chests and trunks on the floor and there are a number of these in the room.

A tongue-and-groove door leads to the next bedroom, at the gable end. Here there is bare thatch also, and two beds. Above one, an iron bedstead, a crucifix has been tucked into the thatch, so it looks down on the sleeper. The other bed is a child's delight though it probably slept an adult. Made of wood, one whole side, facing the wall, is boarded in. The side of the bed is the same shape as the descending thatch. The front is bordered by a band of lace-edged, damask curtain. The room is bathed in light and sunshine through a gable window.

Throughout the house, the walls have been papered, except for the kitchen and dairy. There are religious pictures in all the rooms, and a multitude of calendars in the kitchen. One 'holy picture' in the hallway has been embellished by a border of silver, Oxo-cube wrapping. In the hall also is a coat-rack, the nails covered by wooden thread spools, and boots were tucked into

The distinctive and well-maintained yard is made of carefully picked stones drawn from the beach some seven miles away.

the alcove under the stairs.

To the front the windows look out onto a cobbled yard, with thatched stone and clay buildings facing them opposite. These were and are used for cattle and storage.

Many disused buildings, old and modern, retain a sense of foreboding and emptiness. In this old, clay house, there is a sense of warmth, security, snugness from wind and rain, and a great air of ease and contentment. We don't know all the people who lived in this house, generation after generation, but they have left behind, apart from clay and thatch, a great atmosphere of happiness and goodwill.

Further Reading and Information

Bord Fáilte *Ireland's Traditional Houses* Dublin 1991

Caoimhín Ó Danachair (Kevin Danaher) 'Materials and Methods in Irish Traditional Building' *Journal of the Royal Society of Antiquaries of Ireland* 87, 1957

— 'Some Distribution Patterns in Irish Folklife' *Béaloideas: The Journal of the Folklore of Ireland Society* 25, 1957

Kevin Danaher *The Pleasant Land of Ireland* Cork 1970

— *Ireland's Vernacular Architecture* Cork 1975

Alan Gailey *Rural Houses of the North of Ireland* Edinburgh 1984

Patricia O'Hare 'The Use of Mud as a Building Material: Constructing a Single-Unit Dwelling at Currow, Co. Kerry', *Sinsear: the Folklore Journal*, No. 8, 1995

Patrick and Maura Shaffrey *Irish Countryside Buildings* Dublin 1985

Walter Pfeiffer and Maura Shaffrey *Irish Cottages* London 1990

Linda Watson and Rex Harries (Eds) *Out of Earth: National Conference on Earth Buildings* Plymouth 1995

Arthur Young *A Tour in Ireland 1776–9* London 1780

Useful addresses

Johnstown Castle, Co. Wexford has a fine collection of vernacular furniture. It is open to the public during the summer.

Thatching grants are available from:
The Department of the Environment, Housing Grant Section, Government Offices, Ballina, Co Mayo.

If the building is of exceptional national interest the Heritage Council in Kilkenny may grant aid re-thatching. However, the Council's budget is very limited.

The National Folklore Archive is housed in the Department of Irish Folklore, University College, Dublin.

The National Museum of Ireland, Dublin, has a collection of vernacular furniture which will be on view to the public in the near future.

Centre for Earthen Architecture, Plymouth School of Architecture, Hoe Centre, Notte St., Plymouth, Devon PL1 22AR, UK

Leaflets on building and maintaining clay houses published by Devon Historic Buildings Trust are available from William Burkinshaw, 82 Magdalen Rd Exeter, EX2 4TT, UK